High-speed Trains
for the 21st Century

Colin J. Marsden

Ian Allan
PUBLISHING

Front cover: Forming the 10.02 Paignton–Newcastle service, 'Voyager' set No 220 017 shows off its new CrossCountry livery as it passes Langstone Rock, Dawlish, on 13 May 2008. The new colours had been applied following transfer from Virgin Trains to Arriva, consequent upon the franchise changes of November 2007. *Author*

Back cover: Introduced by First Great Western, the Class 180 'Adelante' units have now started to appear with other operators. The first to be repainted in First Hull Trains livery was set No 180 113, which emerged thus in early April 2009 and is seen passing Chelmscote, near Leighton Buzzard, on 8 April *en route* from Wolverton Works to take up its new duties on the East Coast main line. *Andrew Chambers*

Previous page: As part of 21st-century modernisation Virgin Trains introduced Alstom-built Class 390 'Pendolino' sets on its West Coast route. Forming the 08.45 service from Euston to Glasgow Central, No 390 032 *City of Birmingham* is seen at Barrow Mill, between Carlisle and Penrith, on 9 April 2007. *Brian Morrison*

Left: High-speed rail travel in the 21st century has its roots in the gas-turbine Advanced Passenger Train and diesel-powered High Speed Train projects of the early 1970s. Here the four-car Advanced Passenger Train — Experimental (APT-E) is seen, soon after delivery from Derby in the summer of 1972, on a test run over the BR Research test track at Old Dalby. On 10 August 1975 this futuristically styled train would set a speed record of 152.3mph (245.1km/h) on the Western Region main line between Uffington and Goring. *Author*

First published 2009

ISBN 978 0 7110 3380 1

Published by Ian Allan Publishing

an imprint of Ian Allan Publishing Ltd, Hersham, Surrey KT12 4RG
Printed in England by Ian Allan Printing Ltd, Hersham, Surrey KT12 4RG

Code: 0907/B

Visit the Ian Allan Publishing website at www.ianallanpublishing.com

Introduction

In the mid-1970s, when the first generation of high-speed motive power was introduced in the UK, nobody would have believed that in 2009 the very same trains, albeit thoroughly refurbished, would still be forming the backbone of the country's high-speed rail system.

The High Speed Diesel Train (HST) and to a lesser extent the Advanced Passenger Train (APT), in both its gas-turbine and electric forms, paved the way for future high-speed operations in the UK. However, lack of central funding and overall leadership saw few significant advances until after railway privatisation in the mid-1990s. The principal exception was the electrification in the late 1980s of the East Coast main line and the introduction of locomotive-and-stock formations built to a streamlined profile and with a potential top speed of 140mph (225km/h), and these remain the staple of services between King's Cross and Edinburgh. The other exception was, of course, the introduction in 1994 of the Eurostar service through the Channel Tunnel, using Class 373 trainsets; however, these represented a scaled-down and modified version of the French TGV and for the first nine years of operation were restricted in the UK to a maximum speed of 100mph.

The major advance towards the high-speed trains of the 21st century was made following privatisation, by which time all of the long-distance operators were looking to improve their performance by offering an improved passenger environment and reduced journey times. Virgin Trains, part of Sir Richard Branson's Virgin group, led the field with the announcements of route modernisation for the West Coast main line and the introduction of new high-speed electric and diesel trains for its West Coast and Cross-Country franchises. For the former a top speed of 140mph was envisaged through the use of tilting electric trains, the Alstom-built Class 390 'Pendolinos', while the Cross-Country operation employed 125mph diesel multiple-units built by Bombardier, the Class 220 'Voyagers' and 221 'Super Voyagers', of which the latter were be designed to tilt in order to achieve higher speeds over the most curvaceous sections of route. Subsequently the Bombardier design would be adopted by Midland Main Line for its Class 222 'Meridian' units, introduced on its services from St Pancras to Leicester, Nottingham, Derby and Sheffield, and by open-access operator Hull Trains for the Class 222/1 'Pioneers' used on its high-speed service between King's Cross and Hull.

Another operator to introduce new high-speed trains was First Great Western, which took 14 Alstom-built Class 180 'Adelante' DMUs, capable of 125mph, to supplement HSTs on its services from Paddington. However, these units were to prove troublesome and, following a period in store, have started to appear with other train operators.

The latest operator to introduce high-speed trains is South Eastern, which from 2009 will be using Japanese-built Hitachi Class 395 'Javelin' sets to provide a 140mph service from selected Kent towns to St Pancras International via the UK's only dedicated high-speed line, known as HS1.

The future promises many more high-speed developments with the HST2 or InterCity Express project, which calls for diesel, electric and hybrid train formations to be introduced by around 2015.

Colin J. Marden
Dawlish,
May 2009

Little could anyone have predicted in 1976, when the first production High Speed Trains (HSTs) emerged from the BREL works at Crewe, that more than 30 years later they would still form the backbone of the UK's fleet of high-speed diesel trains. In recent years all operators of the HST fleet have effected major refurbishment, which in the main has not improved the passenger experience, extra aircraft-type seats being crammed into what was once a luxurious travelling environment. Power cars too have largely been refurbished, the vast majority, now operated by First Great Western, National Express East Coast and Arriva CrossCountry, being fitted with state-of-the-art MTU power units in place of the original Paxman Valenta type. On 23 June 2008 First Great Western's No 43122 awaits departure from Plymouth at the head of the 14.06 Paddington–Penzance service. *Author*

Right: Refurbishment and re-engining of the HST power cars operated by First Great Western, National Express East Coast and Arriva Cross Country has been undertaken by Brush Traction of Loughborough, a full overhaul from delivery to return to traffic taking on average around 12 weeks. A number of detail differences exist between each operator's refurbishment; for instance, on First Great Western examples sealed cab-door windows are installed, with an emergency air pocket built into the lower section of the door, while those for National Express and Arriva Cross Country incorporate lockable drop-light cab-door windows. All sport revised head and marker lights, two headlights and two combined marker/tail light units being fitted on either side of the central horn grille. Power cars refurbished and re-engined for National Express and Arriva have also been renumbered with the addition of 200 to the original number. In the summer of 2008, due to a stock shortage, Arriva Cross Country hired in two National Express East Coast sets on Saturdays, and on 19 July, with Brent Knoll as a backdrop, National Express East Coast-liveried No 43238, aided by No 43110 at the rear of the train, was photographed passing the village of Lympsham, Somerset, with the 15.22 Newquay–Manchester Piccadilly service. *Chris Perkins*

HSTs have featured largely in the Cross Country operation since the 1980s, when they were introduced by BR to upgrade North East–South West services. Following rail privatisation in the mid-1990s and the awarding of the Cross Country franchise to Virgin Trains the HSTs were replaced progressively by Class 220 'Voyager' and 221 'Super Voyager' multiple-unit stock. This greatly reduced the number of seats per train, which led to serious over-crowding and much adverse publicity about the quality of the long-distance service provision. Following franchise changes in November 2007 the Cross Country operation passed to Arriva, which upon taking over announced some fundamental changes to rolling stock, the most significant being the leasing of 10 HST power cars and sufficient trailer stock to operate two northbound and two southbound Penzance–Edinburgh corridor services daily. The power cars were all fully refurbished by Brush Traction, the working including the installation of the latest MTU engines, while the trailers were upgraded by Wabtec of Doncaster. The franchise's distinctive new livery of deep maroon and grey was applied to all vehicles, and the first power cars emerged in summer 2008 to be introduced with old-liveried stock on the core long-distance services. Performance since introduction has been exemplary, a high availability figure recorded. Photographed on 22 August 2008, power car No 43301, rebuilt from a derelict No 43101, passes Teignmouth, Devon, on the 08.30 Penzance–Dundee service, at the time the longest through journey possible in the UK. *Author*

Right: In 2007 new operator Grand Central took over a small fleet of six HST power cars to operate a new service between Sunderland and London King's Cross under an open-access agreement. The power cars in question were in poor condition and spent many months under repair at DML Engineering, Plymouth. They retained their original Paxman Valenta engines but received attention which should have rendered them fit for regular service. However, shortly after entry into traffic, which was delayed by late delivery of passenger stock, major technical issues emerged, such that at times only one out of the six was available for service. At one point early in 2008 the operator had to withdraw its service while repairs were effected, while at other times it had to hire trains from other operators in order to provide a skeleton service. Painted in the distinctive black colour scheme, a six-car formation of Grand Central Mk 3 stock led by power car No 43084 and with No 43065 at the rear passes Pelaw on 2 March 2008 during an empty-stock movement from Heaton to Sunderland. *Ken Short*

Left: In the spring of 2008 a start was made on repainting the HST power cars and trailer stock retained by East Midlands Trains. Although upgraded, the power cars did not to receive new engines, instead retaining refurbished Paxman VP185 units. Power car No 43058 is illustrated passing Cossington on 15 September 2008 at the rear of the 14.30 Nottingham–St Pancras. The year was one of transition in terms of the liveries worn by EMT's principal fleets of HST and 'Meridian' stock, the erstwhile Midland Mainline livery gradually being replaced by the new colours of blue and white with the familiar Stagecoach 'swirl' on the cab ends. *John Binch*

Left: It was back in the days of British Rail's InterCity sector that the East Coast's Class 91 'racehorses' were introduced, when, under the auspices of Managing Director John Prideaux, they entered service on the newly electrified main line. Photographed on 23 May 1995 sporting full InterCity 'swallow' livery, No 91 002 *Durham Cathedral* awaits departure from King's Cross at the head of the 09.10 to Leeds. *Author*

Below: Although many enthusiasts would have preferred to have seen diesel trains operating on the East Coast route, the introduction of the Class 91s and Mk 4 stock greatly improved the quality of service and paved the way for massive growth in rail travel. On 25 June 1996, led by No 91 031 *Sir Henry Royce*, the 08.00 King's Cross–Edinburgh races through Doncaster. *Author*

Above: Under the privatisation of the railways the East Coast franchise was awarded to Sea Containers, trading as Great North Eastern Railway (GNER). The company continued to operate the Mk 4 and Class 91 formations but re-liveried the fleet in dark blue offset by red doors and bodyside band. Looking very impressive at full speed, a set of GNER-liveried Mk 4s headed by a Driving Van Trailer (DVT) is seen passing Colton Junction, south of York, on 23 June 2005. *Author*

Below: GNER blue-liveried Mk4 DVT No 82206 speeds through Barkston South Junction on 30 May 2006 at the head of a southbound express. Note the dome on the DVT's roof, indicating that the coaching stock was equipped with wi-fi internet access. *Brian Morrison*

Right: In GNER days the Class 91s were refurbished and reclassified as '91/1s'. Sporting GNER blue livery and a stick-on name, No 91 131 *County of Northumberland* heads north past Brookmans Park on 4 August 2007. *Jamie Squibbs*

Although built with a design speed of 140mph, the Class 91s are limited to 125mph in normal service. The class did, however, make headline news on 2 June 1995, when No 91 031 and a shortened set of Mk 4 stock achieved a speed of 154mph (247.8km/h) at both Tollerton, north of York, and Tallington, north of Peterborough. Carrying its name in the form of a transfer applied to its GNER blue livery, sister locomotive No 91 029 *Queen Elizabeth II* passes Harringay on 1 June 2007 at the head of the 11.30 King's Cross–Leeds service. *Author*

Along with the Mk 4 carriage stock, the entire fleet of Class 91 locomotives is allocated to Bounds Green depot in North London, from where they dominate services from King's Cross to Leeds, Newcastle, Edinburgh and Glasgow, working alongside a handful of HST sets retained for services to destinations beyond the electrified network. Led by Mk 4 DVT No 82230 and propelled by Class 91 No 91 119 (out of view at the rear), the 10.00 service from Glasgow Central to King's Cross via Edinburgh heads across Slateford Viaduct on 28 February 2005. *Chris Perkins*

Left: Night photography using digital equipment is often quite difficult to achieve, images often turning out with unpleasant colour-casts, but an adjustment to the white balance usually corrects this problem. This beautifully exposed night shot features three GNER Class 91s — Nos 91 117, 91 120 and 91 122 — at King's Cross on 4 November 2007. *Stacey Thew*

Above: Early in 2007 Sea Containers, owner of GNER, agreed to surrender the franchise of the East Coast route, and a new bidding process commenced,

the winner being National Express, which took over the franchise with effect from 9 December. The operation was rebranded as National Express East Coast, and the original GNER branding was quickly removed, initially in favour of a white bodyside band upon which the National Express name was applied, and ultimately by a completely new livery. Passing Langford, near Biggleswade, on 10 August 2008, National Express-branded Class 91 No 91 117 *Cancer Research UK* powers the 13.30 Sunday service from King's Cross to Edinburgh. *Brian Morrison*

Above: In recent years all Class 91 refurbishment and classified repairs have been undertaken at Doncaster Works, firstly by Bombardier Transportation and latterly by Wabtec Engineering. Following the reallocation of the East Coast franchise at the end of 2007 overhauls have seen locomotives outshopped in the very pleasing standard National Express livery of all over silver/grey offset by a broad angled band with stylised National Express name in blue and red. The locomotive number appears in white on the cab side, the last two digits being repeated on the front end in black on the yellow panel on the non-driving side. No 91 111 is seen at Doncaster Works before returning to traffic. *Derek Porter*

Right: As a result of the difference in maintenance schedules between National Express locomotives and rolling stock it was initially rare to find the new-liveried Class 91 and Mk 4 coaches working together. However, even coupled with the trailer sets in National Express-branded GNER blue the trains looked impressive. On 22 September 2008 No 91 111 brings up the rear of a southbound East Coast service arriving at Peterborough. In the locomotive-stabling siding on the left can be seen an EWS Class 67 on 'Thunderbird' duty. *John Binch*

Delivered in 1993 and introduced in service in 1994, the Class 373 fleet, working the new Channel Tunnel services to and from mainland Europe, immediately became the new icon of high-speed rail travel in the UK, although it would be more than 10 years, with the opening of High Speed 1 rail link through Kent, before the full potential of these 186mph (300km/h) trains could be realised. This photograph records the historic moment, on 20 June 1993, when the first Eurostar set — Nos 3001/2 — were delivered to North Pole depot. They were hauled through the Channel Tunnel by French diesel locomotives, following which they were uncoupled to allow this picture to be taken of No 3001 emerging from the tunnel portal. *Author*

Between the introduction of Eurostar services in 1994 and commissioning of the first section of British high-speed line (HS1) in September 2003 the Eurostar sets could travel at their maximum speed of 186mph (300km/h) only in France and Belgium. Making an impressive sight racing through northern France, French-operated Eurostar set Nos 3229/30, forming the 09.27 Waterloo International–Brussels, pass Watterdam on 12 August 1997. *Author*

Upon its launch in 1994 the Eurostar service included a single intermediate stop at Ashford International, providing a direct link from Kent to mainland Europe. Originally the station was used by trains traversing the domestic lines from London through Kent, but in the early years of the 21st century, when the High Speed 1 line was under construction, major works were carried out to build a high-speed flyover above part of Ashford station and to connect the International platforms with the high-speed route. Drawing its power from the third rail, French-operated set No 3227 traverses the down main line at Ashford at the head of the 12.53 Waterloo International–Paris on 6 September 1995. Following the opening of the new high-speed line through Kent and terminating at St Pancras International the Eurostar sets have had their third-rail 750V DC power-collection equipment removed. *Author*

As built the Eurostar trainsets were designed to draw power from the UK's 750V DC third-rail supply, France's 25kV AC overhead and Belgium's 3,000V DC overhead. Following agreement to operate sets to destinations in Southern France and the French Alps some French-owned sets were additionally equipped to collect power from a 1,500V DC overhead supply, and this has allowed some interesting off-route workings to be recorded. As part of the launch of a new Waterloo International–Avignon service in 2002 a special demonstration run was arranged for the British media and travel trade. Here empty stock for the return journey on 10 April, comprising set Nos 3209/10, is seen *en route* from Paris Le Landy depot to Avignon; the train is pictured traversing 'classic' French tracks through Orange, where it would have been drawing power from the 1,500V DC network. The return run to London would make use of the new high-speed TGV line which had only recently opened. *Author*

334.7 km/h

Above: As part of construction of the UK's high-speed line (HS1) through Kent the International platforms at Ashford station were electrified at 25kV AC while retaining their third-rail supply. Running on AC power after traversing the first section of HS1, opened in 2003, Eurostar set No 3020 arrives on 23 June 2006 at the head of the 09.09 Waterloo International–Paris Nord. *Author*

Inset: Prior to the formal commissioning of HS1 a series of high-speed runs was undertaken using set Nos 3313/4, intended originally for the abortive North of London services. On 30 July 2003 they were used to transport a small party of British rail and national press for a record-breaking journey over the new line, working initially from Waterloo International to a location near Folkestone before making two high-speed runs. On one of these, passing Kilometre-post 60.4 at 11.35am, the train set a new UK speed record of 208mph (334.7km/h) — an achievement conveyed to passengers by means of this screen relaying the view from the driver's cab. *Author*

Coincidental with the official opening of the full length of HS1 Eurostar transferred its London terminus from Waterloo to St Pancras, where rebuilding of the original station had taken several years to complete, the original Barlow trainshed now housing the new Eurostar terminal, and a new domestic station, for use by East Midlands Trains and South Eastern Trains being added on to the original structure. The rebuilt station was opened officially on 14 November 2007, the revised service offering a significant reduction in travelling times between London and Brussels or Paris due to the vast majority of the route being authorised for full 186mph (300km/h) running. In addition to that at Ashford a new intermediate station was opened at Ebbsfleet, and these are due to be joined by a third, at Stratford, in time for the 2012 London Olympic Games. This view features three Eurostar trains at St Pancras on the evening of the opening day, when members of the travelling public enjoyed their first taste of ultra-high-speed rail travel in the UK. *Author*

The Eurostar fleet, owned jointly by British, French and Belgian administrations, was, once all sets had been delivered, found to exceed traffic requirements, business growth and thus passenger numbers not being as high as originally forecast. The surplus led to three French-operated sets' being decommissioned from the Eurostar pool and used for French domestic services on the Lille–Paris corridor, in the process being rebranded 'TGV' and losing their yellow front ends and third-rail power-collection equipment. However, Eurostar now anticipates that within the foreseeable future these sets will be needed back in the core fleet, as the increase in passengers following the transfer of operations to St Pancras is likely to require the provision of extra trains. This view features French TGV Eurostar No 3228 at Paris Nord on 4 June 2006. *Author*

Originally maintenance for the British Eurostar fleet was undertaken in purpose-built accommodation at North Pole depot in West London, but the transfer of the London terminus to St Pancras rendered this location unsuitable. A new depot was therefore built on redundant railway land at Temple Mills, East London, and this is reached by means of a spur from the high-speed line near Stratford. The new depot, which in addition to maintaining the British-owned fleet carries out programmed maintenance for the French and Belgian sets, comprises a single-ended shed spanning eight tracks (each line able to accommodate a full 20-car formation) and further buildings for heavy maintenance and stores. Here three Eurostar sets share depot space on 24 June 2008. *Author*

Left: In terms of domestic services the major advance towards the high-speed trains of the 21st century was made in the wake of railway privatisation, Virgin Trains leading the field with the introduction of new high-speed electric and diesel trains for its West Coast and CrossCountry franchises. For the latter it ordered a fleet of 125mph diesel multiple-units built by Bombardier, the Class 220 'Voyagers' and 221 'Super Voyagers', of which the latter were designed to tilt in order to achieve higher speeds over the most curvaceous sections of line. Here 'Super Voyager' No 221 118 *Mungo Park*, forming the 14.25 Plymouth–Edinburgh Waverley, passes South Brent as on 20 April 2007. First-class accommodation was provided in one driving car, identifiable by a yellow band applied to the coupling cover. *Author*

Above: Construction of the 38 four-car and 40 five-car Class 220 and 221 units was undertaken jointly by Bombardier Transportation plants in Brugge, Belgium, and Wakefield, Yorkshire, the former building the greater number. In the Brugge plant a pre-formed GRP nose section is seen awaiting installation by sliding over the strengthened cab-end framework. Note the cleanliness of the facility. *Author*

Left: All members of 'Voyager' and 'Super Voyager' fleets were named, this being the result of a directive issued by Virgin Trains Managing Director Chris Green, who was a great believer in the importance of public relations in promoting the business and its service. One of a number of ceremonies saw the final set, No 221 144, named *Prince Madoc* at Bombardier's Central Rivers depot on 14 October 2002. Chris Green is second from left. *Author*

Left: Being totally new, in both its tilting and non-tilting form, the 'Voyager' design required extensive testing in order to obtain the type approval necessary for it to carry passengers in the UK. Some testing of both variants was carried out in Belgium and in France. In January/February 2002 the first of the tilting sets, No 221 101, running as a four-car formation, was tested in France on the curvaceous section of line between Cahors and Brive, being seen here crossing the impressive Souillac viaduct on 1 February. *Author*

Above right: Both British- and Belgian-built sets were tested in the UK after delivery, initially on the lightly used freight-only line towards Monk Bretton from Crofton, where a 'temporary' depot (still in use today) was built. On 1 March 2001 set No 220 016, with its number applied in white on the red bodywork as an experiment, passes Walton on a test special from Crofton. *Author*

Right: In a scene unlikely to be repeated, 'Super Voyager' No 221 101 *Louis Bleriot* departs Brive, France, *en route* to La Mons for further tests, during which 125mph would be achieved for the first time by a Class 221. On the left is 1977-built SNCF '72xx' 1,500V DC B-B electric No 7262 awaiting departure with the 16.17 service to Paris (Gare d'Austerlitz). *Author*

Left: While the 'Voyager' formations looked impressive from the outside, the poor reliability of the service combined with passenger dissatisfaction over the interior design (notably the paucity of luggage space) soon attracted criticism. Here 'Super Voyager' No 221128 *Captain John Smith*, forming an Edinburgh–Plymouth service, passes Duffield, north of Derby, on 23 April 2004. *Author*

Above: The last four Class 221 'Super Voyagers' were built as four-car units, principally for operation over the North Wales Coast route, but in time they would be found all over the operating area. On 23 April 2004 No 221 142 *Matthew Flinders* passes Stenson Junction, between Derby and Burton-upon-Trent, on a Newcastle–Bristol service. *Author*

Left: Forming the 06.16 Preston–Plymouth service on 6 April 2006, Class 221 'Super Voyager' No 221 125 *Henry the Navigator* races down the bank from Whiteball Tunnel as it heads from Somerset into Devon. When the units were being designed it was claimed that, with 750hp available to each vehicle, on-line failures would be rare, sufficient power being available to complete a journey even if two engines were to fail. In reality this has not usually been the case, and in the event of engine failure sets are normally withdrawn from service, and trains cancelled. *Author*

Above: Forming the 08.25 Penzance–Dundee, No 220 008 *Draig Gymreig / Welsh Dragon* — identified as a standard, non-tilting 'Voyager' by its silver Virgin badge and red-backed nameplate — passes Silverton, between Exeter and Tiverton, on 8 June 2005. The provision of a four-car set was totally inadequate on this service, known to be one of the busiest of the day. *Author*

Above: Virgin 'Voyagers' were introduced progressively from 21 May 2001, replacing firstly locomotive-hauled stock (powered by Class 47s and Class 86s) and then HSTs. However, they had to overcome a number of teething troubles, ranging from water ingress to the electronics when travelling along the sea wall at Dawlish in rough weather to tilt problems on the Class 221 fleet, but the Bombardier support engineers performed miracles, and the fleet soon settled down to give an acceptable miles-per-casualty figure. On 28 August 2002 Nos 221 105 (running as a four-car set) and 220 013 approach Carlisle on the 09.18 Brighton–Edinburgh Waverley service, travelling via the West Coast route. On the right is Freightliner Class 47/0 No 47 292. *Author*

Right: Prior to the introduction of the 'Voyager' types stock it was necessary to 'clear' a number of diversionary routes for the operation, as nature of the routes covered and the extent of ongoing engineering work meant that diversions from the booked routes would be commonplace. This presented Network Rail with a considerable amount of work but proved very useful. One diversionary route is the Avonmouth branch, which has to be used if the main route between Bristol Parkway and Bristol Temple Meads is out of bounds. Here 'Super Voyager' No 221 122 *Doctor Who* approaches Avonmouth station on 25 June 2004 as the 06.26 York–Plymouth, diverted from its normal route due to major engineering work at Filton Abbey Wood. *Chris Perkins*

Right: The standard design of nameplate for a non-tilting 'Voyager' was a plain cast plate with a red background. Produced by Newton Replicas, the plates were attached by four bolts. All names would be removed upon reallocation of the Cross Country franchise to Arriva. *Author*

Left: In common with the 'Pendolino' units and the first batch of Class 57/3 locomotives all 'Voyager'-type units received a cast 'Virgin' plate on the cab front. Tilting stock had plates with a red background, non-tilting being identified by a silver background. Like the nameplates, the shields would be removed upon transfer of the fleet to Arriva Trains. *Author*

Right: Class 221 nameplate design, incorporating the 'Super Voyager' legend at the top. These plates were finished with a dark blue background. Some were quite large, depending on the length of the name. *Author*

Left: One of the busiest stations on the Virgin Trains network was Manchester Piccadilly, used by both West Coast and Cross-Country franchises. On 24 July 2002 'Super Voyager' No 221 131 *Edgar Evans* stands alongside a Class 158 'Express' DMU, having recently arrived on a through service from Brighton via Gatwick Airport, Kensington Olympia, Reading, Birmingham and Stafford. *Author*

Above: The core business routes for the Cross-Country operation were identified by Virgin as Bristol–York and Manchester–Reading, 'arms' to such destinations as Edinburgh, Glasgow, Penzance, Brighton, South Wales and Bournemouth being regarded secondary and catering mainly for the leisure market. On 28 August 2002 'Super Voyager' No 221 136 *Yuri Gagarin* departs Sheffield as the 06.45 Bristol Temple Meads–Newcastle, while on the left a Midland Main Line HST awaits departure for St Pancras. *Author*

Above: The nature of their work sees the Class 220s and 221s passing through some of the most beautiful countryside in the UK. Here an unidentified 'Super Voyager' forming the 06.05 Edinburgh–Plymouth service crosses Blachford Viaduct, near Ivybridge, on 14 July 2005. *Author*

Right: One of the world's most-photographed railway locations, Dawlish, on the South Devon coast, is the location for this view, recorded on 30 January 2008, after Arriva Trains had taken control of an expanded Cross-Country operation. Devoid of nameplates and cab-front logo but sporting the new 'Cross Country' branding, five-car 'Super Voyager' No 221 140 on the 07.24 Derby–Plymouth passes similar No 221 135 forming the 08.30 Penzance–Dundee. *Author*

Left: Mixed pairings of a 'Voyager' and 'Super Voyager', providing a nine-car formation —albeit lacking a through connection throughout the train, which caused problems if only one 'shop' (buffet) was open — were commonplace at weekends and on the busiest services. On 16 September 2007, just before Arriva took on the franchise, 'Voyager' No 220 004 *Cumbrian Voyager* and 'Super Voyager' No 221 136 *Yuri Gagarin* were photographed passing Churchill & Blakedown signalbox, on the Kidderminster line, with a Newcastle-bound service diverted due to Sunday engineering work. The train would regain its normal routeing at Birmingham New Street. *Chris Perkins*

Right: A major re-branding exercise was needed following the reallocation on 11 November 2007 of the Cross-Country operation from Virgin Trains to Arriva. The latter elected to trade as simply 'Cross Country', which name at first appeared in the form of bodyside stickers applied to the existing colours, but in the spring of 2008 it embarked upon a programme to re-livery the units (Nos 220 001-034 and 221 114-141) transferred. The first to be treated — at Central Rivers depot, using high-quality transfers — were the Class 220s, the operation taking most of the summer to complete, after which a start was made on the '221s'. Sporting the new livery of deep maroon, pink and silver, No 220 026 departs Paignton on 17 June 2008 as the 16.15 Paignton–Newcastle. *Author*

Left: While certainly not being intended for high-speed passenger operation, a fleet of Class 57/3 locomotives was employed by Virgin Trains to rescue failed 'Voyager'-type units, as well as to haul Class 390 stock over non-electrified lines. Company policy dictated that staff at all depots be instructed in the necessary procedures, and to this end a number of '57/3'+'Voyager' formations were to be seen engaged on training duties. On 13 January 2005 No 57 304 *Gordon Tracy* was used to haul No 220 033 *Fife Voyager* on a number of runs between Plymouth and Newton Abbot, the combination being seen passing Aller as the 12.45 Newton Abbot (Hackney Yard)–Plymouth. *Author*

Right: While travelling over the East Coast and West Coast main lines the 'Voyagers' are able to exploit the full potential of their 125mph maximum speed. In the days when Virgin held the Cross-Country franchise the Class 221 'Super Voyagers' were authorised for tilting operation on the West Coast and on a small section of the Oxford–Birmingham route, but following the changes of November 2007 the Arriva sets have not operated over the northern section of the WCML, and tilting operation has been largely isolated, although the sets remaining with Virgin West Coast retain this capability. Among the latter is No 221 110 *James Cook*, seen passing Colton South Junction, south of York, on the 10.58 Bristol Temple Meads–Newcastle service on 23 June 2005. *Author*

Left: Forming the 08.45 Bournemouth–Manchester Piccadilly service, 'Super Voyager' No 221 129, devoid of its *George Vancouver* nameplates and with interim 'Cross Country' branding on its existing Virgin Trains livery, approaches Southampton Central on 25 February 2008. The Cross Country route from Birmingham to Bournemouth via Reading and Southampton has an approximately hourly daytime service in each direction. *Author*

Above: Following the division of the Class 221 fleet in the autumn of 2007 a total of 16 'Super Voyager' sets (Nos 221 101-113/142-144) remained with Virgin Trains West Coast for operation of services between London and North Wales. These sets, which retain their original names and cast nose-end plaques, are still allocated to Central Rivers depot, near Burton-upon-Trent, but receive daily maintenance at regional depots on the West Coast route. Forming the 11.28 Euston–Llandudno, No 221 113 *Sir Walter Raleigh* passes Milton Keynes Central on 19 February 2008. *Author*

Left: On 6 September 2008, the Gloucester–Bristol Parkway route being closed for engineering work, all Cross-Country services were diverted via the Chepstow line. Forming the 10.25 Derby–Paignton, 'Voyager' No 220 029 takes the tunnel route at Severn Tunnel Junction, having travelled via Chepstow and reversed at Newport. The area beyond the train was once occupied by Severn Tunnel Junction diesel depot. *Chris Perkins*

Above: Arriva's new Cross Country livery deep maroon (which in some lights looks more like brown), complemented by a silver body, black window surrounds, pink doors and yellow ends, is well suited to the 'Voyager' body profile and, and offset by a large stylised 'XC' on the cab sides, looks impressive at speed. While the train operators would like to run longer trains this is not possible with the number of sets available, so it is still rare to find sets working together except on the busiest services at weekends in the high season. On 26 July 2008 sets Nos 220 007 and 220 002, forming the 06.10 Derby–Paignton, take the centre road through Dawlish Warren. *Author*

Left: The second operator in the UK to introduce 'Voyager'-type trainsets was Midland Main Line, the sets in question being Class 222 'Meridian' units employed on services from St Pancras to Leicester, Nottingham, Derby and Sheffield. They were formed originally in four-, five- and nine-car sets, but the four-car sets were soon found to be inadequate to meet burgeoning passenger demand. Changes were swiftly authorised, one car being taken from each nine-car set to strengthen some four-car sets to five vehicles, and following franchise changes in November 2007 the remaining four-car sets were re-formed by reducing the eight-car sets to seven. In the days of four-car formations No 222 013 departs Derby as the 14.20 to St Pancras on 21 January 2005. *Author*

Above: Due to changes in the franchise requirement some of the longer sets were stored after delivery to the UK from Bombardier in Brugge; all sets are now operational, but major changes have been effected, five- and seven-car trainsets having been formed to meet passenger demand on the St Pancras–Nottingham/Sheffield routes. On 27 February 2008, at which time some sets consisted of eight coaches, No 222 002 passes Loughborough on the 08.55 St Pancras–Nottingham service. *Author*

CITY OF SHEFFIELD

Left: Still running as an eight-car formation on 27 February 2008, set No 222 002 storms past Cossington, south of Loughborough, on the 13.55 St Pancras–Nottingham. All 23 'Meridian' sets are allocated to Derby Etches Park depot, where in 2008/9 major expenditure was incurred in developing the facility, which included installation a synchronised lifting system. The Class 222s are non-tilting units but are built to the same body profile as the 'Voyagers', this being dictated by the fact that fleet was a follow-on order to the Virgin build, and re-jigging Bombardier's Brugge factory would have been both costly and time-consuming. *Author*

Left, inset: In Midland Main Line days a small number of 'Meridian' sets were given names appropriate to the route. This was the stick-on name applied to No 222 004. *Author*

Right: Running as a five-car set, No 222 015 heads south at Cossington on 25 February 2008 as the 14.07 Nottingham–St Pancras. The Class 222s have a maximum design speed of 125mph, which is authorised on selected sections of the Midland route south of Trent Junction. Performance and reliability of these sets is good, and passenger perception of the fleet seems to be higher than that of their Virgin equivalents. This is likely to be the result of a much-improved interior design, giving the impression of more space. *Author*

Above and right: As part of the changes of November 2007 Midland Main Line gave way to East Midlands Trains, the franchise having been won by Stagecoach. For the launch of the operation on 11 November five-car set No 222 017 was outshopped in its new operator's colours of white, blue, red and orange and shown off to the media at Nottingham before working a special to St Pancras via Derby. These photographs show it prior to departure from Nottingham and following arrival at the state-of-the-art St Pancras, adjacent to the original station, which now serves as the London terminus for Eurostar services. *Author*

Above: The third operator to opt for 125mph 'Voyager'-type trainsets was FirstGroup subsidiary Hull Trains, an open-access operator providing services between King's Cross and Hull. The sets in question were four-car Class 222/1s built in Brugge by Bombardier; identified as 'Pioneers', they replaced Class 170 DMUs that had proved inadequate in terms of both meeting passenger demand and maintaining speeds sufficient to blend in with East Coast operations. Forming the 08.12 Hull–King's Cross, No 222 101 *Professor George Gray*, allocated to Crofton and painted in a pleasing livery of green, grey and gold, passes Harringay on 21 July 2008. *Brian Morrison*

Right: 'Pioneer' No 222 102 *Professor Stuart Palmer* storms through Hitchin on 10 August 2008 while working the 10.12 Sunday service from Hull. These sets have a maximum speed of 125mph and as configured for Hull Trains provided seating for 33 First- and 170 Standard-class passengers, the First-class end of the train being identified by a yellow strip on the coupling cover and another at cantrail height. Hull Trains converted to full Class 180 operation in early summer 2009, the Class 222 sets being transferred to East Midland Trains. *Brian Morrison*

Left: One of the most significant investments in new rolling stock in the history of Britain's railways came as a result of privatisation and Virgin Trains' modernisation of the West Coast main line. The entire existing fleet of locomotive-hauled Mk 2 and Mk 3 stock, powered by a diverse selection of Class 86, 87 and 90 electric locomotives, was replaced by a fleet of 53 tilting 'Pendolino' electric sets built in Italy and fitted out at Alstom, Washwood Heath, Birmingham. They entered traffic in the period 2001-5 and are officially allocated to Alstom's depot in Manchester, but receive additional maintenance at Wembley and Polmadie. Built as eight-car sets, they were strengthened to nine-car formations soon after delivery, and further Government funding will see them running as 11-car sets by 2014. Four additional units have also been authorised. This was the view inside the main test hall at Alstom, Washwood Heath, on 29 April 2004, with set No 390 006 on the left and No 390 047 on the right. *Author*

Designed for a maximum speed of 140mph but restricted to 125mph pending the installation of full in-cab signalling, the 'Pendolino' units operate all services on the route from Euston to Birmingham, Wolverhampton, Manchester, Liverpool, Carlisle and Glasgow/Edinburgh, on which their tilting capability enables them to provide a much faster service than is possible with conventional trains. Since 2002 various localised speed restrictions have been in force as a result of ongoing infrastructure improvements being implemented by Network Rail, but from 2009 the full potential of these sets should become apparent. Painted Virgin Trains' striking livery of silver, red, and black, No 390 014 *City of Manchester* passes Cathiron, on the outskirts of Rugby on 20 April 2007, on a southbound express. Note the red-backed Virgin plaque affixed to the front end. *Jamie Squibbs*

Above: During the period of operation as 'short' eight-car sets, No 390023 *Virgin Glory* heads north past Lower Hatton, on the West Coast main line between Stafford and Crewe, forming a Euston–Liverpool Lime Street service on 14 July 2003. The 'Pendolino' sets usually operate with their First-class accommodation at the London end of the train. *Chris Perkins*

Right: The old order and the new side by side at Manchester Piccadilly on 16 December 2002. On the left stands 'Pendolino' No 390 014, forming a special media train from Euston, while on the right is Class 87 No 87 026, providing the propelling power for the 13.30 service to Euston. *Author*

Above: Another photograph taken during the period of transition on the West Coast main line, featuring an immaculate 'Pendolino' and an aged Mk 3 set posing under the roof at Manchester Piccadilly on 23 July 2002. The 'Pendolino', No 390 010, had formed a special from Birmingham International and was named *Commonwealth Games 2002* as part of the ongoing media campaign promoting both the new trains and the Manchester-based Games. *Author*

Left: Each 'Pendolino' set has two pantograph-fitted trailer vehicles, marshalled as the third vehicle from either end of the train. In service only one has its pantograph raised at any one time, in order to avoid wire bounce. This is car No 69527 from set No 390 027. *Author*

Left: Contrast in front-end design. The 21st-century high-speed icon that is the 'Pendolino' stands alongside a Mk 3 Driving Van Trailer at Manchester Piccadilly. *Author*

Below: Behind the streamlined front cowl of the 'Pendolino' is a retractable Dellner auto-coupler which allows sets to be coupled together, but they are not used as such in normal service. However, the couplers have frequently been used to attach to Class 57/3s for diversionary routeing and, until the end of 2008, for operation over the North Wales route between Crewe and Holyhead. With its cover slightly out of position, revealing part of the coupler, set No 390 022 *Penny the Pendolino* approaches Milton Keynes Central on a service to Euston while sister No 390 021 *Virgin Dream* awaits departure on a northbound service bound for Liverpool Lime Street. *Author*

Descending Beattock Bank as the 06.46 Euston–Glasgow Central, the first northbound departure of the day, nine-car set No 390 042 *City of Bangor / Dinas Bangor* passes Kirkton, between Crawford and Abington, on 6 April 2006. All 'Pendolino' trainsets received names while under construction; in the main these either had 'Virgin' prefixes or recognised cities on the line of route. However, a number have been subsequently renamed in support of charity events, book launches etc. *Chris Perkins*

Left: Between Queen's Park and Harrow & Wealdstone in North London two very contrasting forms of rail transport run side by side, the West Coast main line running parallel with London Underground's Bakerloo Line, and if lucky a photographer can capture the two train types in a single shot. A suitable overbridge exists between South Kenton and Kenton, from which this view of 'Pendolino' No 390 008 *Virgin King*, forming the 13.03 from Euston to Crewe, was recorded on 13 October 2007. Heading in the opposite direction is a Bakerloo Line train on its way from Harrow & Wealdstone to Elephant & Castle. *Brian Morrison*

Above: A major drawback of the body profile necessary to allow tilting operation is the premium it places on interior space. A maximum of 147 First- and 300 Standard-class passengers can be accommodated in a nine-car 'Pendolino', compared with 154 First- and 420 Standard-class in a typical locomotive-hauled Mk 3 formation. During the changeover period many passengers continued to opt for the latter, which had a less claustrophobic interior, in both First and Standard class, with much more comfortable seating and better toilets. Against this, the new trains offered a smoother and quicker journey, better air-conditioning and a power supply at each seat.

On 23 January 2007 the final set of the original build, No 390 053 *Mission Accomplished* calls at Crewe on the 16.46 Euston–Edinburgh Waverley. *Chris Perkins*

Above: In July 2006 Virgin Trains had 'Pendolino' set No 390 029 *City of Stoke-on-Trent* outshopped as a mobile billboard to publicise the cinema release of Warner Bros' film *Superman Returns*, starring Brandon Routh, Kevin Spacey and Kate Bosworth. Combining scenes from the film with Virgin Trains branding, the livery was applied at Alstom's Wembley Traincare Depot and at the time represented the highest-profile external advertising yet seen on a domestic inter-city train in the UK. Forming a northbound service, the unit is pictured passing Cathiron, north of Rugby, on 2 July 2007. *Jamie Squibbs*

Right: Two 21st-century high-speed trains run side by side at Carstairs on 11 July 2008. On the left Virgin West Coast 'Pendolino' No 390 011 *City of Lichfield*, forming a delayed Euston–Glasgow Central service, passes EWS Class 67 No 67 029 on a 'Northern Belle' charter from Euston to Helensburgh Upper. The 30 Class 67s are the only twin-cab diesel locomotives in the UK capable of 125mph. Built following railway privatisation, they have never fulfilled their full potential, the Royal Mail contract for which they were ordered having been lost, and despite an expensive and long-drawn-out certification process to allow them to run at 125mph they are now generally limited to 100mph. *Andrew Cook*

Left: The area around Rugby, including the junctions north of the station, where the Trent Valley line and that to Coventry and Birmingham diverge, has seen major infrastructure work as part of the West Coast Route Modernisation scheme, resulting in a virtually new station, extra platforms, greater route capacity, smoother junction flows and higher speeds. For much of the period 2004-8 speed restrictions and route diversions were in force, creating some interesting photographic opportunities. On 18 January 2005 'Pendolino' set No 390 005, forming a Euston–Wolverhampton service, heads away from the Rugby stop while a pair of Freightliner Class 66s, No 66 515 nearer the camera, look on from the north-facing bay platform. *Chris Perkins*

Left: The northern section of the West Coast Anglo-Scottish route passes some splendid scenery, and locations such as Shap and Beattock are particularly popular with photographers. Here 'Pendolino' No 390 005 *City of Wolverhampton*, forming the 10.15 Euston–Glasgow Central, crosses the River Clyde at Crawford on 6 April 2006. *Chris Perkins*

Above: In terms of the driver's environment alone the 'Pendolino' design represented a major culture change from the previous locomotives and DVTs. The cab was designed very much with the driver's workload in mind, all controls being located in logical and easily viewed positions. Just visible on the left of the picture is the combined power/brake controller, pulled back to apply power and pushed forward for braking, while beyond it is the Train Management System (TMS) display, which provides the driver with information on almost all aspects of the state of the train. *Author*

Left: Following rail privatisation Great Western Trains sought new high-speed trains to supplement its existing fleet of HSTs. Various manufacturers were invited to tender for what was to become Class 180, Alstom coming up with the winning bid to supply 14 five-car 'Adelante' sets derived from its 'Coradia 1000' product range. Bodyshells were fabricated in France and fitted out at Washwood Heath, Birmingham, where the body for one of the driving cars for set No 180 103 is seen in the main shop. *Author*

Right: By the time of the new trains' arrival Great Western Trains had been re-branded as 'First Great Western'. This photograph was taken at Bristol St Philips Marsh depot on 25 July 2001, when Class 180 was shown to the media for the first time and FirstGroup's new 'Barbie' livery was launched. 'Adelante' No 180 103 poses alongside HST power car No 43029, the latter masquerading as 43001 — a number allocated originally to one of the prototype HST power cars. Sadly the 'Adelante' units were to prove very unreliable and by comparison with HSTs offered passengers a poor travelling environment. *Author*

Left: Allocated to Old Oak Common depot in West London, the 'Adelante' sets, with a maximum speed of 125mph, were allocated to selected services, mainly semi-fast and stopping trains, from Paddington to Cardiff, Bristol, Worcester and Oxford. Pictured alongside an HST formation (with power car No 43024 nearer the camera), set No 180 106 awaits departure from Cardiff Central with the 09.55 to Paddington on 25 June 2002. *Author*

43001

First

Above: The great Brunel trainshed at Paddington plays host to the new order of Great Western high-speed travel on 4 March 2004. On the left 'Adelante' set No 180 109 prepares to depart as the 15.03 to Cheltenham while on the right No 180 113 makes ready to form the 15.15 to Bristol Temple Meads. *Author*

Right: The 'Adelante' sets were never intended for the West of England route, but in the autumn of 2004 Exeter-based crews were trained on their operation to permit their use on services from Paddington to Exeter (and one to Plymouth). However, the type had first appeared west of Exeter on Saturday 22 May 2004, when set No 180 113 formed the 10.05 Paddington–Paignton service and 14.46 return, the latter train being seen pulling off the Paignton branch at Aller. *Author*

Left: The Paddington–Worcester route always featured largely in the Class 180 roster, the type's standard formation of five cars (four Standard and one First) satisfying passenger demand. Devoid of its coupling cover, set No 180 104 comes off the Evesham branch and trundles past Norton Junction signalbox while on a Paddington–Hereford service on 2 September 2008. *Jack Boskett*

Above: From the autumn of 2004 the 'Adelante' sets were introduced on additional Paddington–Exeter semi-fast trains, which for the first time in many years provided stations such as Slough, Theale and Hungerford with a through service to and from the West. Forming the 11.55 Exeter St Davids–Paddington, set No 180 104 passes Rewe, between Exeter and Tiverton, on 13 April 2006. *Author*

Left: Regular daytime operation of Class 180s west of Exeter was confined to a few weeks in the summer of 2004, when Exeter-based staff were being trained on the type and the 14.35 Paddington–Plymouth consisted of a 10-car formation. On 5 August Nos 180 107 and 180 101 were photographed heading towards Kennaway Tunnel, Dawlish. *Author*

Above: On the busiest London–Bristol/Cardiff services pairs of 'Adelante' sets were used, providing seating for 84 First- and 452 Standard-class passengers. On 19 November 2004 a 10-car formation comprising Nos 180 101 and 180 114 passes Manor Farm, Cholsey, *en route* from Paddington to Cardiff. Withdrawn by First Great Western between 2007 and 2009, the Class 180s are now in service with First Hull Trains and Northern Rail and will soon commence operation with National Express and Grand Central. *Chris Perkins*

Above: The latest high-speed trains to arrive in the UK are the first four Class 395 'Javelin' sets, built in Japan by Hitachi Industries. These are due to be introduced from June 2009 on domestic services between St Pancras and various destinations in Kent over the HS1 high-speed route and during the 2012 London Olympics will be employed on services between St Pancras and Stratford. This photograph shows the first driving car for set No 395 001 being off-loaded at Southampton Docks on 23 August 2007. *Author*

Right: The Class 395s are some of the most complex trains in the world, being able to draw power from the from 25kV AC overhead supply on HS1 as well as from the traditional 750V DC third rail, while in terms of signalling they are equipped with the TVM430 cab signalling used on HS1 as well as being compatible with more conventional signalling systems found elsewhere. The driving cab reflects this complexity as well as the current trend of having a combined power/brake controller operated by the driver's left hand. *Author*

Left: In spring 2008 the first 'Javelin' delivered, No 395 001, departs Ashford on the 'classic' line towards Tonbridge on an early test run to check the operation of the 750V DC power-collection equipment and the standard BR Automatic Warning System. Although the unit was at this stage painted in all-over blue with white 'Hitachi' branding, a more sophisticated livery is expected to be applied before the type's introduction to normal service. *Brian Stephenson*

Above: Since their arrival in the UK the first four 'Javelin' units, housed in new purpose-built depot accommodation at Ashford, Kent, have been tested on both DC and AC lines, reaching their maximum design speed of 140mph (225km/h) on HS1 and 100mph (160km/h) on domestic lines. On the second evening of testing in multiple, Nos 395 001 and 395 002 approach Beechbrook Farm as train 5Z91, the 20.16 Ashford International–Wennington Crossovers, on 23 July 2008. *Brian Stephenson*

One of the greatest strengths of the Hitachi design lies in its quality, every last detail being taken care of by a dedicated maintenance and commissioning team from Japan based in the UK. Extensive testing of the four pre-production sets is intended to resolve any teething troubles, allowing necessary modifications to be incorporated in the construction of the main batch of 25 due for delivery from late 2009, while the first four will be suitably upgraded in the UK before entering normal service. On 31 August 2008 sets Nos 395 001 and 395 002 are seen near Charing while on a driver-training run from Ashford to Swanley and then to Ramsgate and Faversham. *Brian Stephenson*